GOTHIC ORNAMENT

EDITED BY
CAROL BELANGER GRAFTON

DOVER PUBLICATIONS, INC.
MINEOLA, NEW YORK

The CD-ROM in this book contains all of the images. Each image has been saved as a high-resolution JPEG, an Internet-ready JPEG, and a TIFF. There is no installation necessary. Just insert the CD into your computer and call the images into your favorite software (refer to the documentation with your software for further instructions).

Within the "Images" folder on the CD you will find three additional folders—"High Resolution JPG," "JPG," and "TIF." Every image has a unique file name in the following format xxx.JPG. The first 3 characters of the file name correspond to the number printed with the image in the book. The last 3 letters of the file name, JPG, refer to the file format. So, 001.JPG would be the first file in the JPEG folder.

Also included on the CD-ROM is Dover Design Manager, a simple graphics editing program for Windows that will allow you to view, print, crop, and rotate the images.

For technical support, contact:
Telephone: 1 (617) 249-0245
Fax: 1 (617) 249-0245
Email: dover@artimaging.com
Internet: **http://www.dovertechsupport.com**
The fastest way to receive technical support is via email or the Internet.

NOTE

Over 500 architectural and decorative elements are featured in this exquisite collection of ornamentation from the Gothic era (1150–1500). Depicted in architecture, sculpture, and paintings Gothic style flourished in Western and Central Europe. Cathedral and churches were built as giant stone structures with tall steeples reaching up to heaven. Interior designs included carved masonry and woodwork, ornate ironwork, frescoes and stained glass. Gargoyle statues on the exterior were commonplace and were believed to ward off evil spirits. This treasury of engravings includes a variety of designs from the period including floral and foliate motifs, capitals, borders, brackets, friezes, grotesques, and other medieval flourishes.

003

001

002

004

005

1

006

007

008

009

010

011

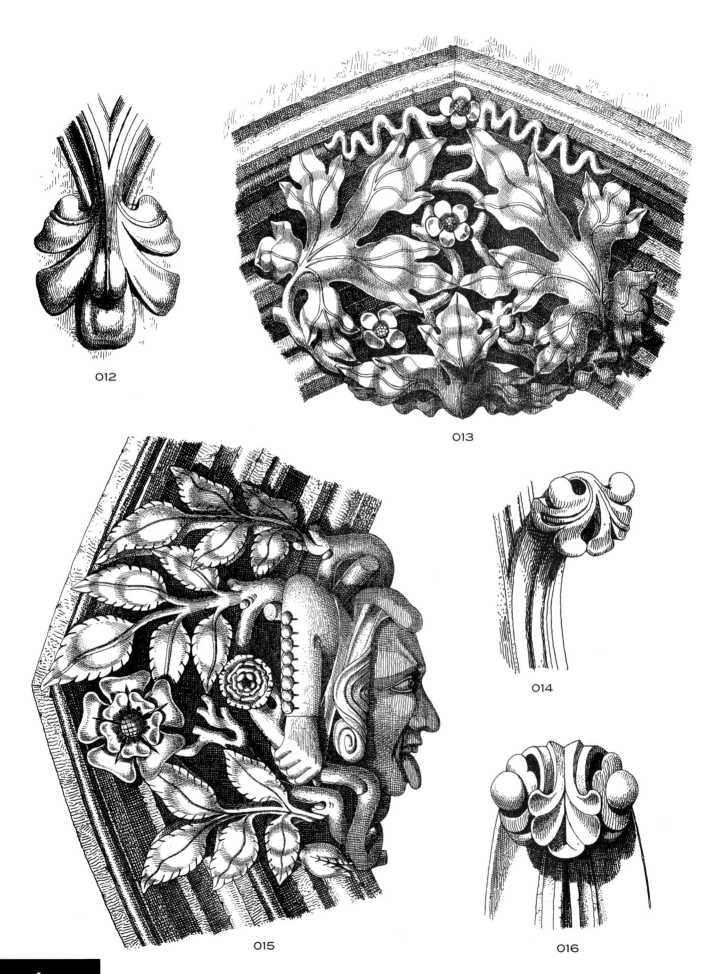

012

013

014

015

016

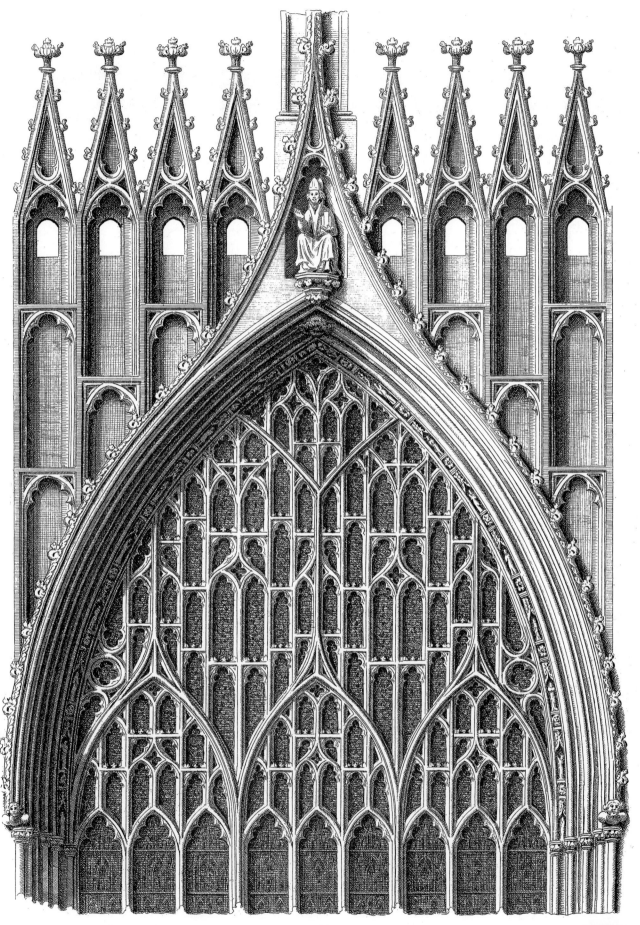

018

019

020

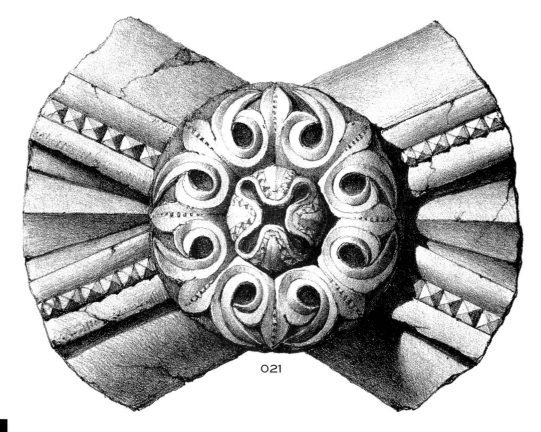

021

6

022

023

024

7

025

026

8

027

028

029

030

031

9

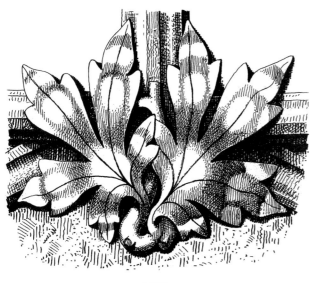

032

033

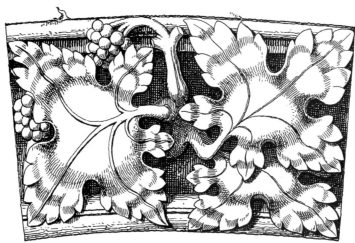

034

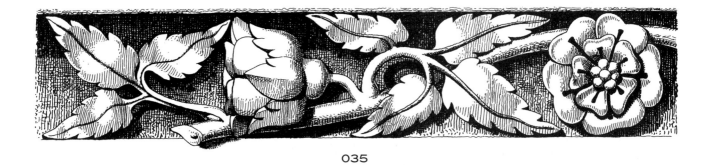

035

036

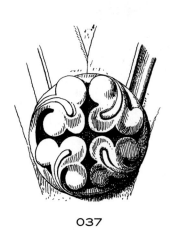

037

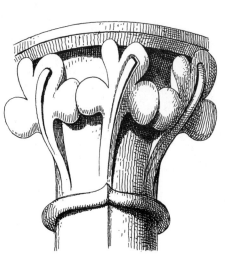

038

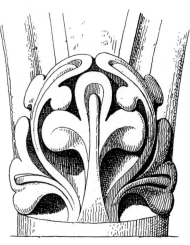

039

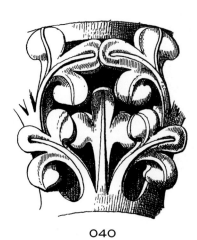

040

041

042

043

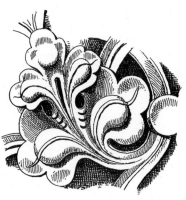

044

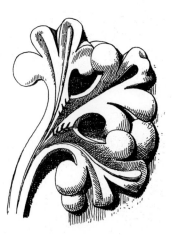

045

046

047

048

049

050

051

052

053

054

13

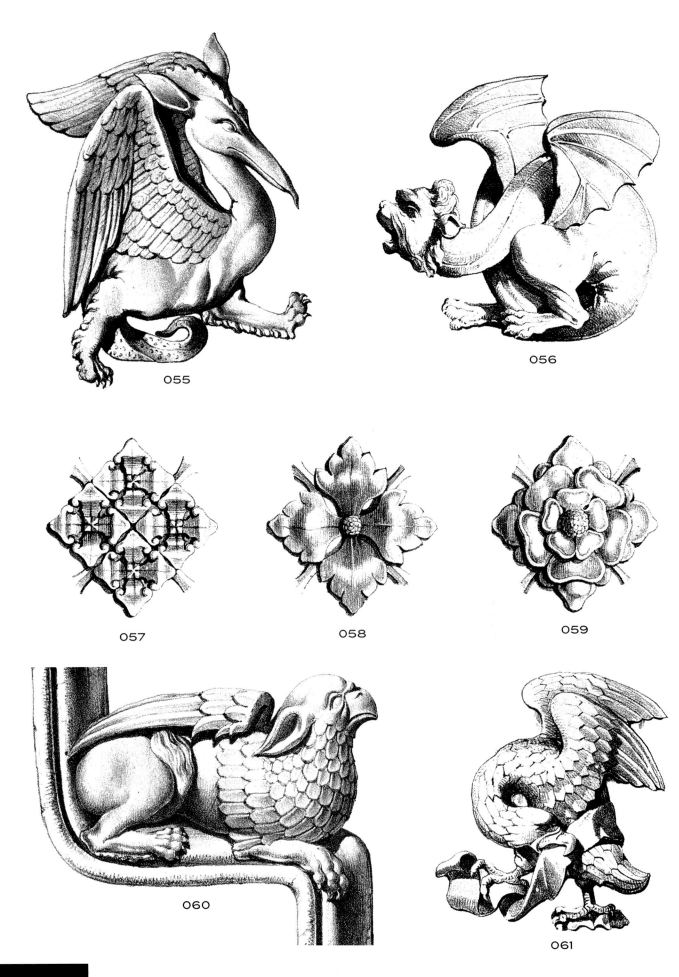

055

056

057

058

059

060

061

14

15

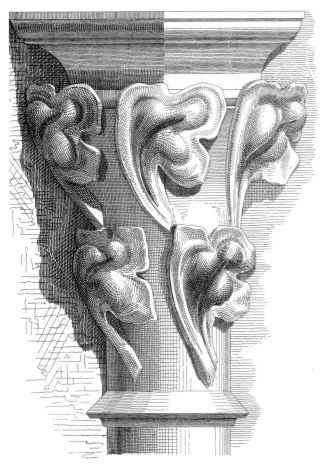

063

064

065

16

066

067

068

069

070

071

072

073

074

075

076

077

078

079

080

081

082

083

084

085

086

087

088

089

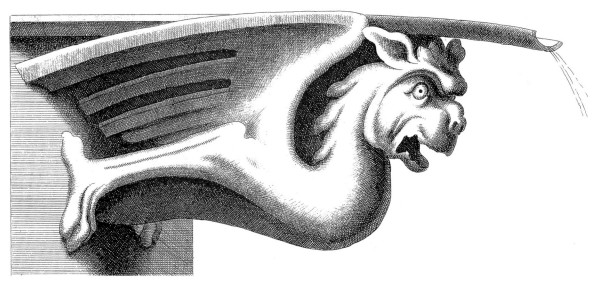

090

091

23

092

093

094

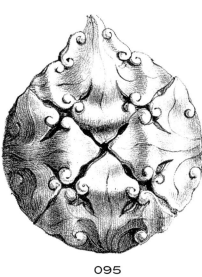

095

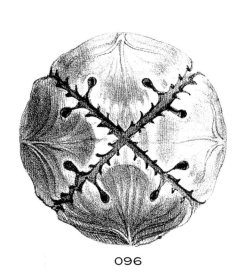

096

097

098

099

100

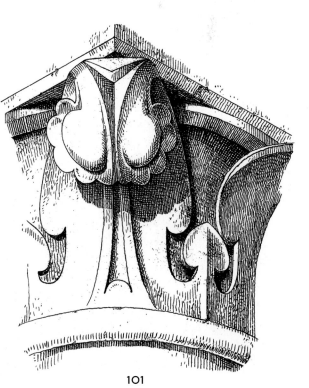

101

25

102

103

104

105

106

107

108

109

110

111

112

113

114

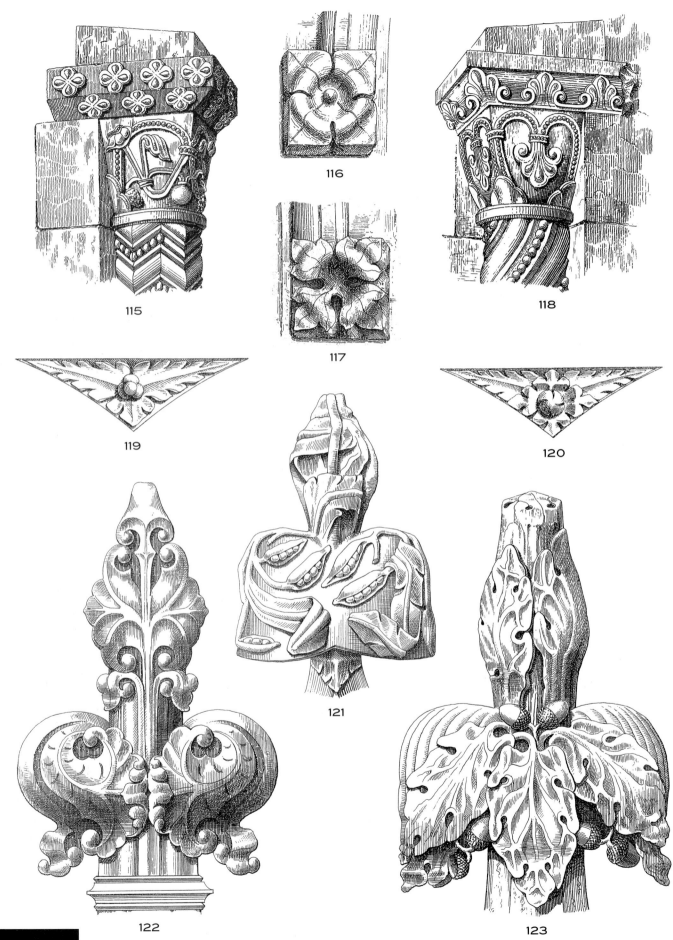

115

116

117

118

119

120

121

122

123

124

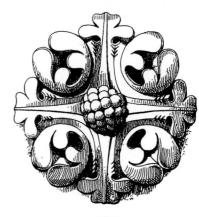

125

126

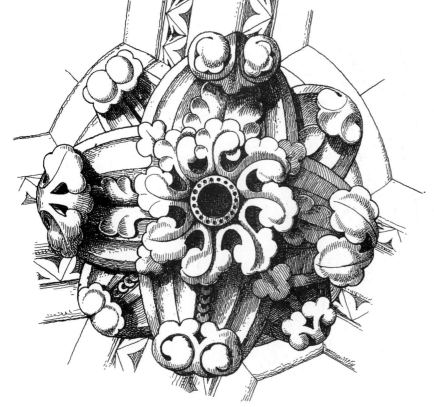

127

128

30

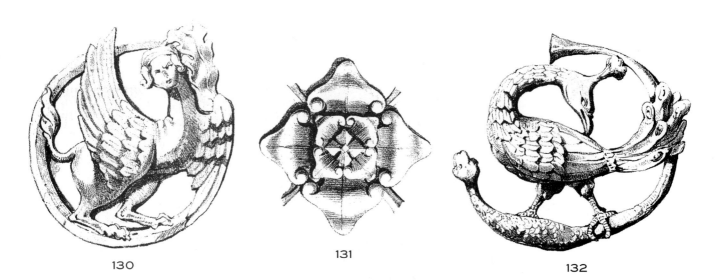

130

131

132

133

134

135

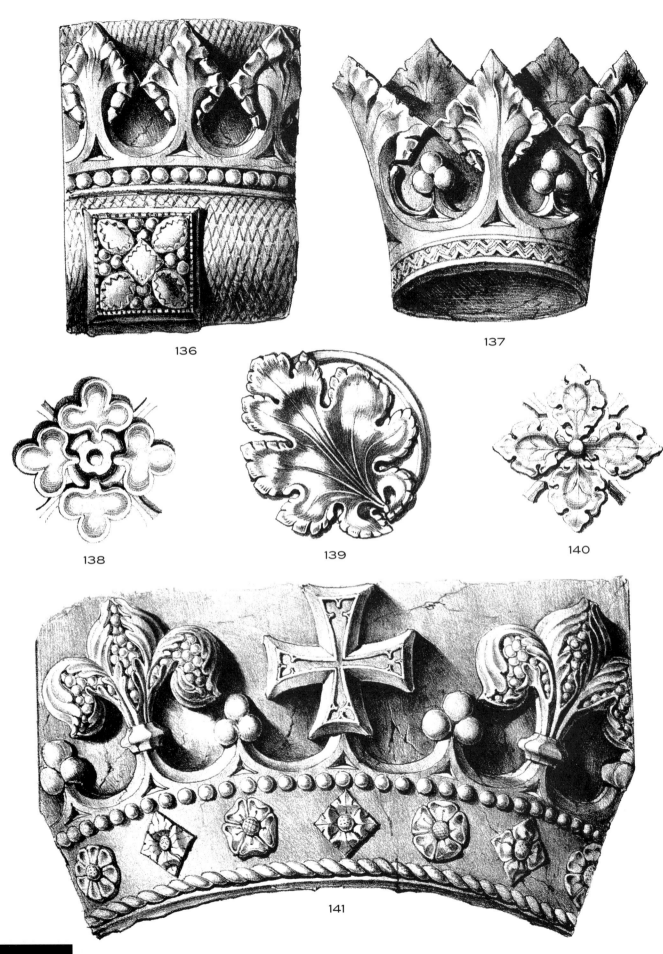

136

137

138

139

140

141

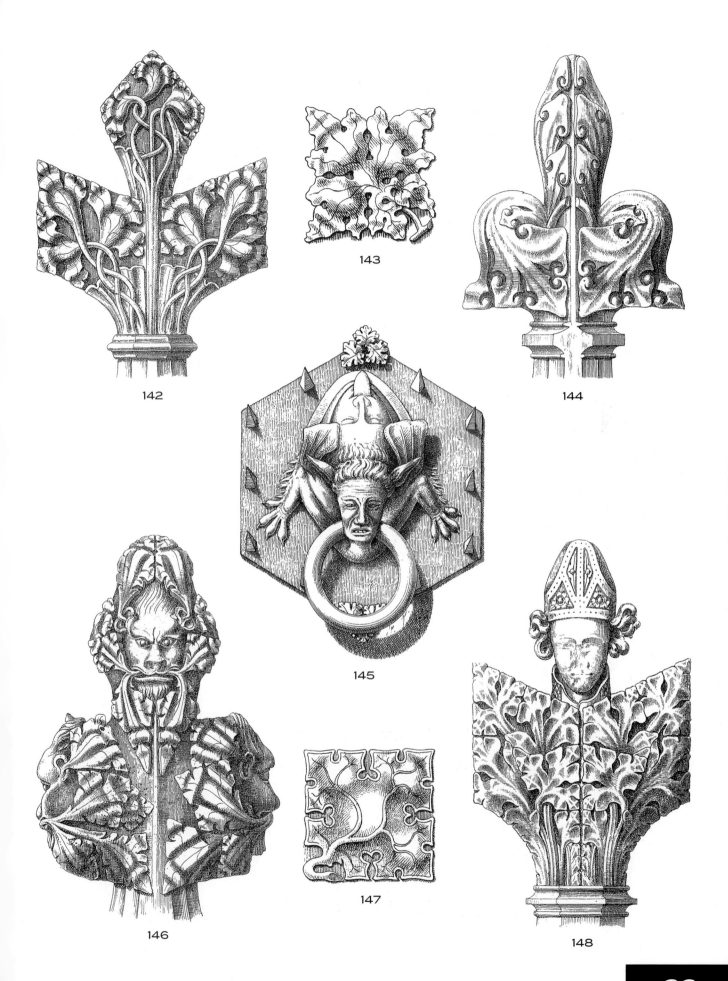

142

143

144

145

146

147

148

149

34

150

151

152

153

154

155

156

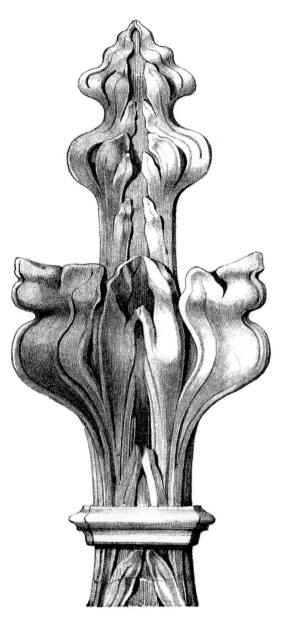

158

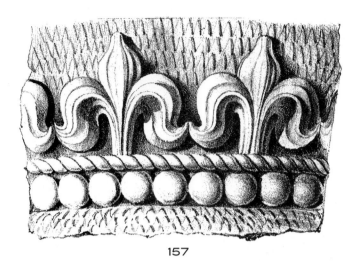

157

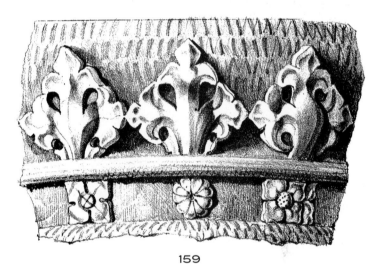

159

160

37

161

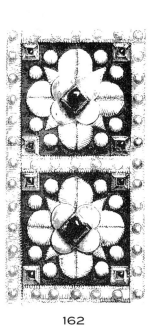

162

163

164

165

166

167

168

170

171

172

173

174

175

176

41

177

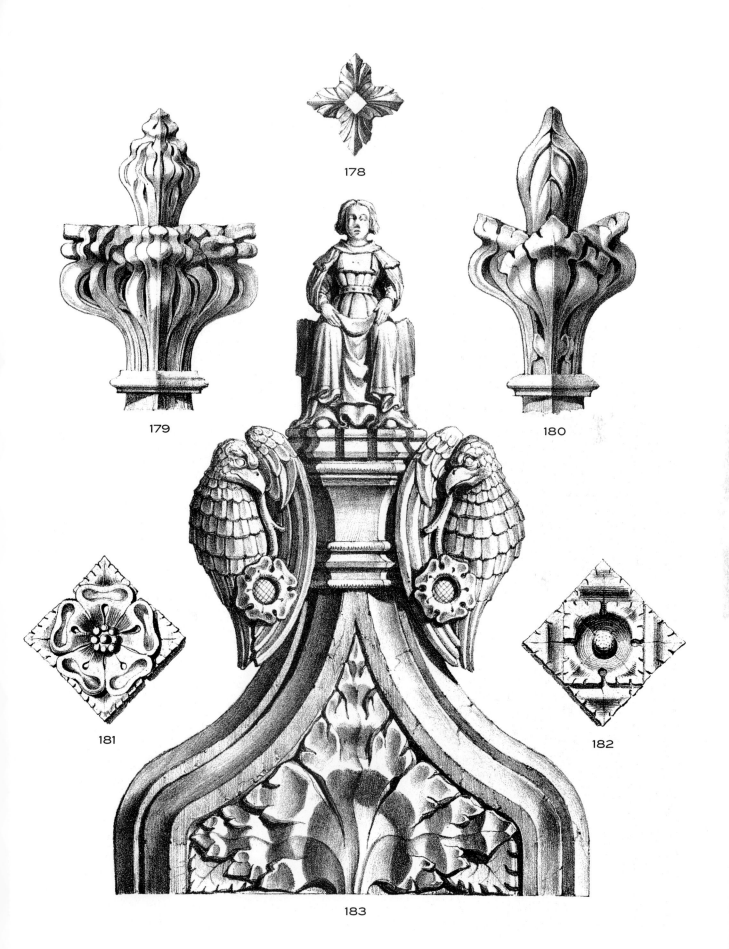

178

179

180

181

182

183

184

185

186

187

188

189

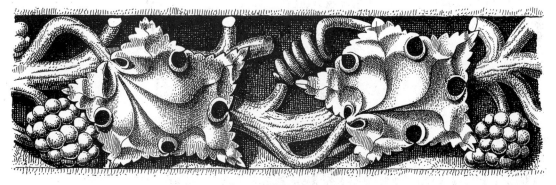

190

191

192

193

194

195

196

197

46

198

199

200

201

202

203

204

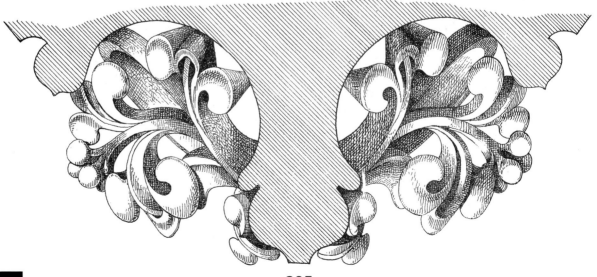

48

205

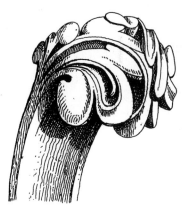

206

207

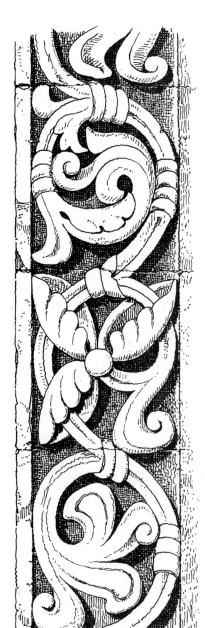

208

209

210

211

212

213

214

215

216

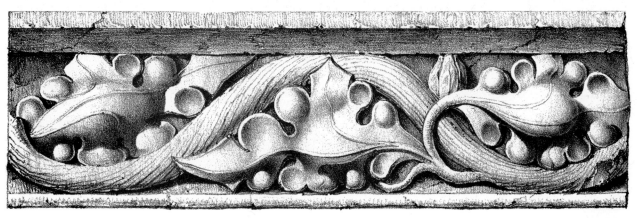

217

52

219

220

221

222

223

224

54

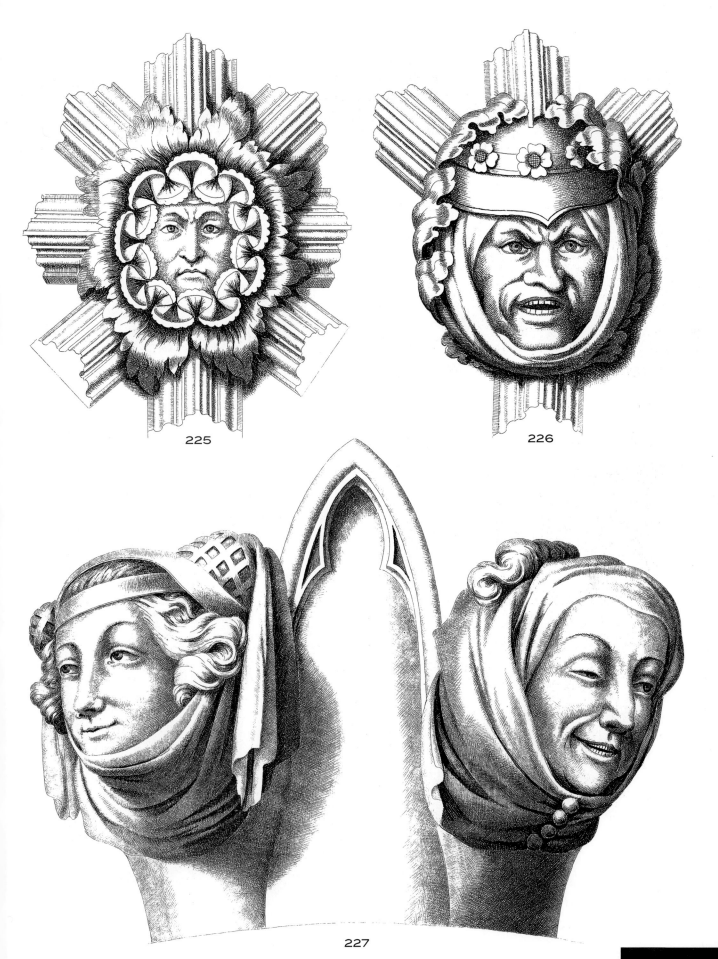

225

226

227

228

229

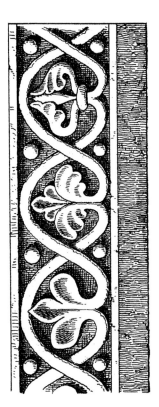

230

231

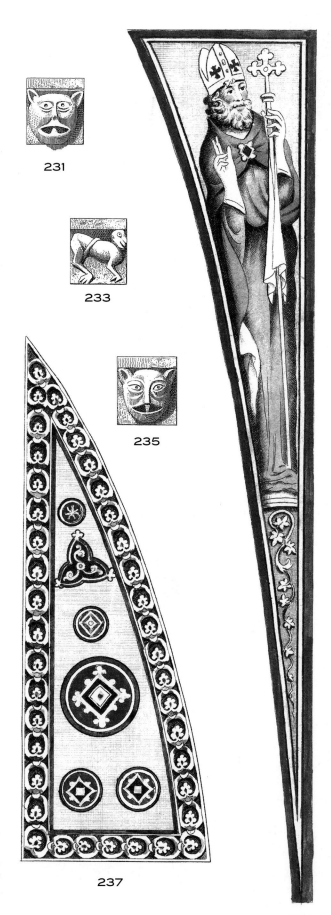

233

235

237

238

239

232

234

236

240

57

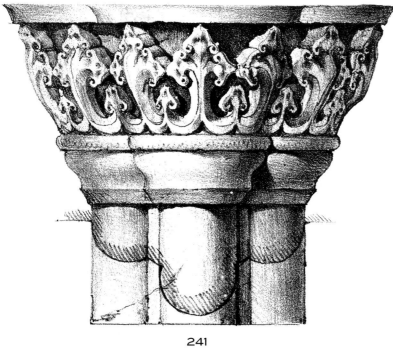

241

242

243

244

245

247

248

249

250

251

252

253

254

255

256

257

258

259

260

261

262

263

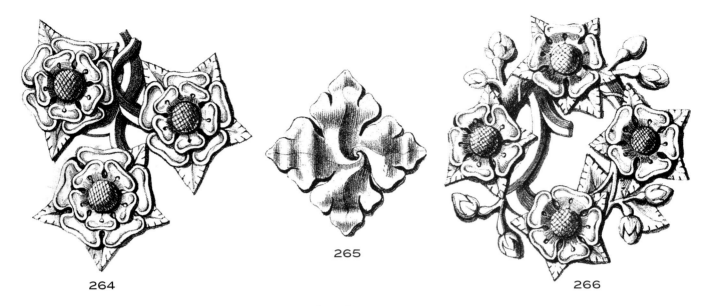

264

265

266

267

268

269

270

271

272

273

274

275

276

277

65

278

279

280

281

282

283

284

285

286

287

288

289

290

291

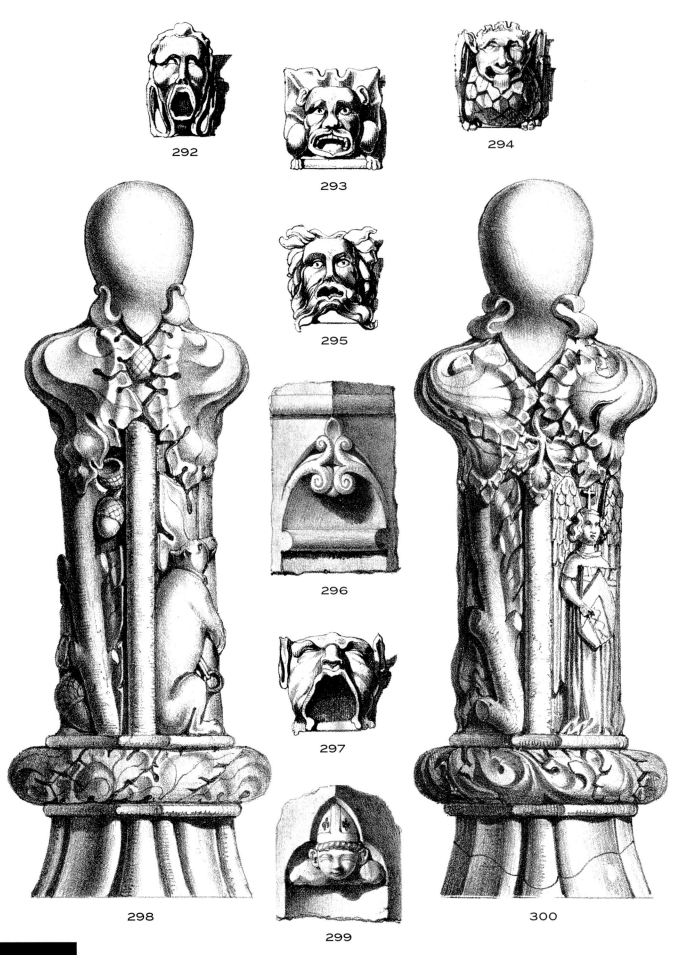

292

293

294

295

296

297

298

299

300

301

302

303

304

305

306

307

308

309

310

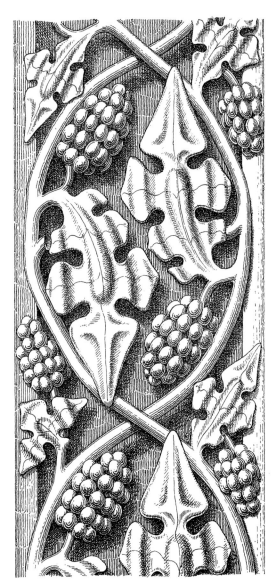

315

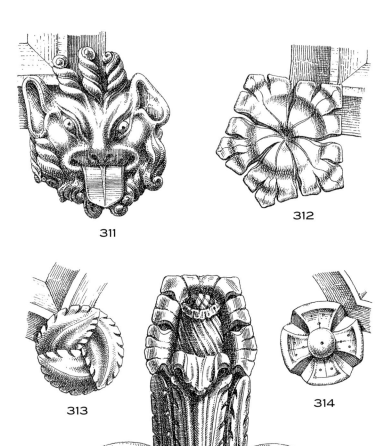

311

312

313

314

316

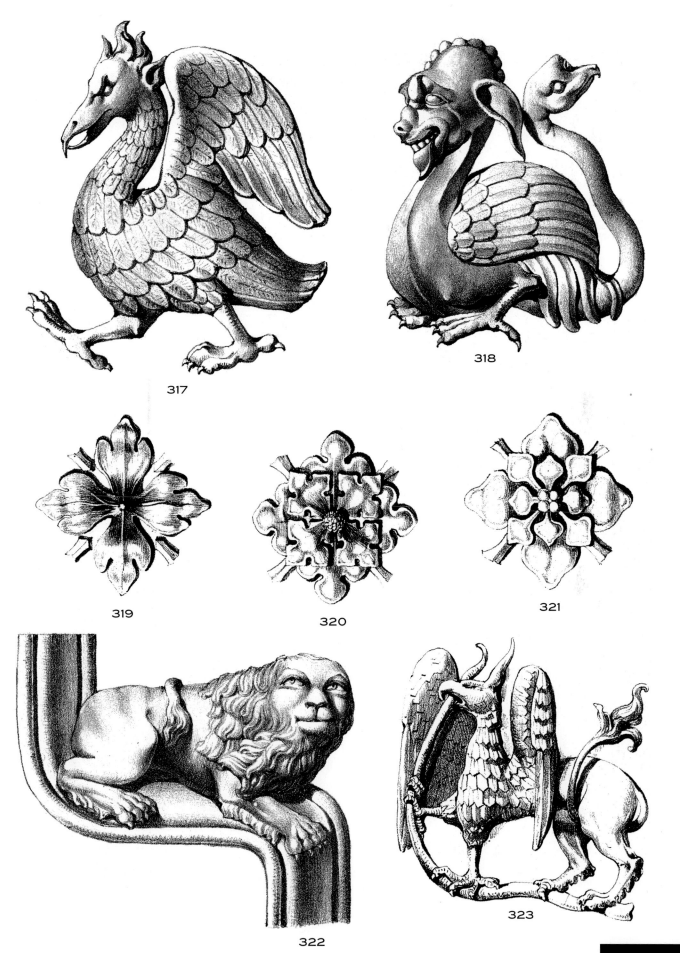

317

318

319

320

321

322

323

324

325

326

327

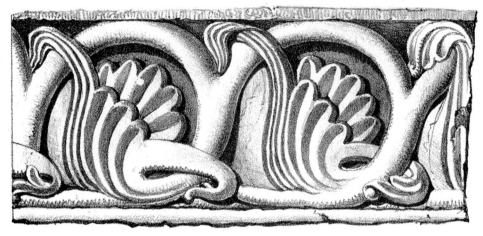

328

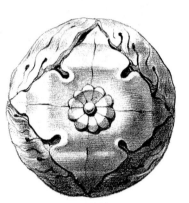

329

330

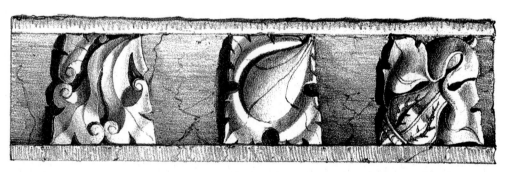

331

332

333

334

335

336

337

338

339

340

341

342

343

344

345

346

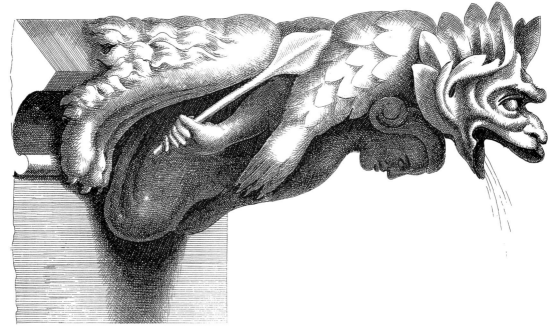

347

348

349

350

351

352

353

354

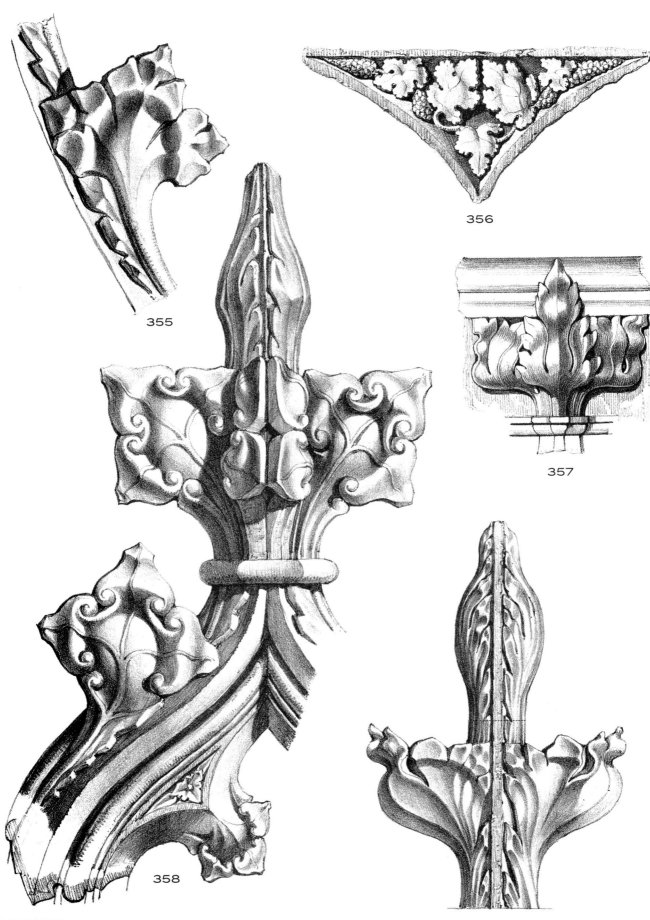

355

356

357

358

359

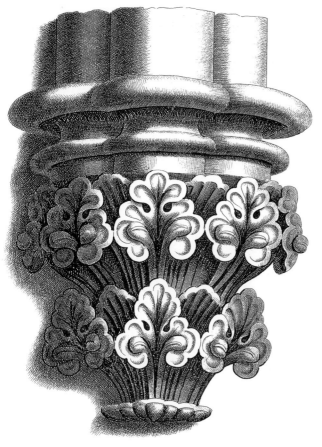

360

361

362

363

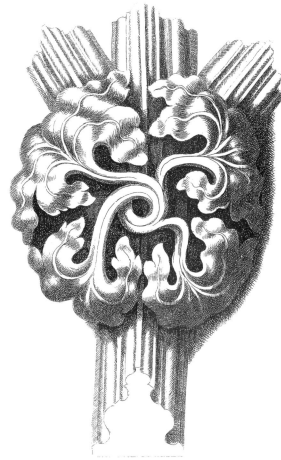

364

365

366

367

83

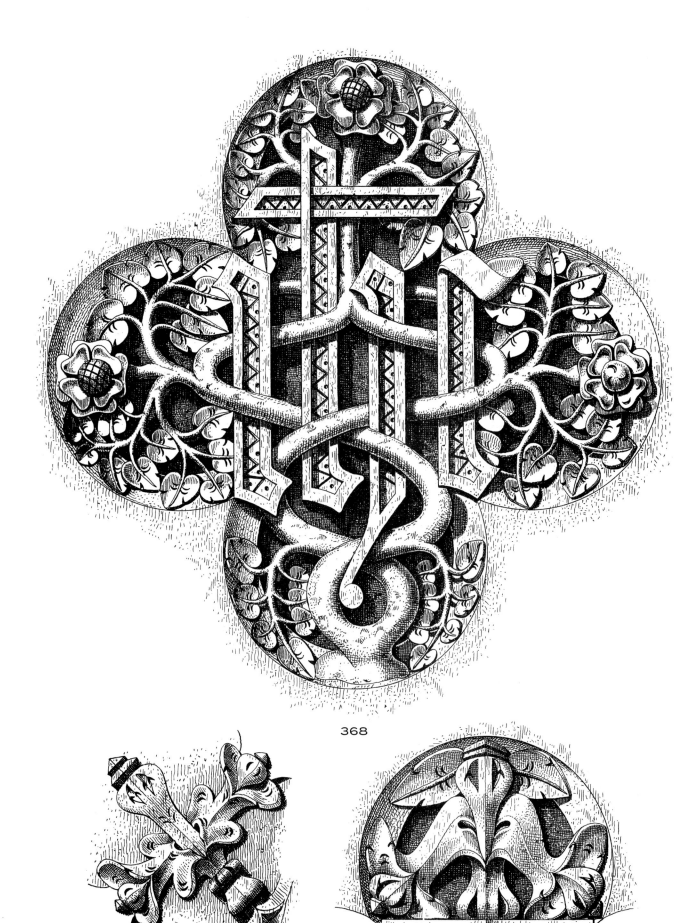

368

369

370

371

372

373

374

375

376

377

85

378

379

380

381

382

383

384

385

386

387

388

389

390

391

392

393

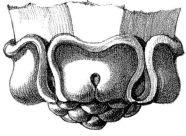

394

395

396

397

398

399

90

400

401

402

403

404

405

406

407

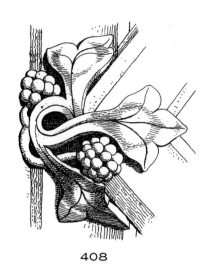

408

409

410

411

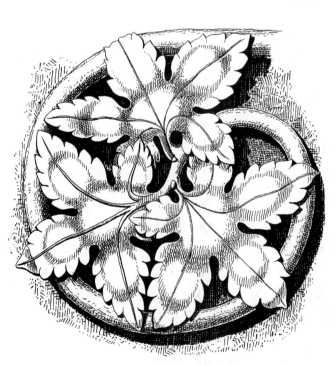

412

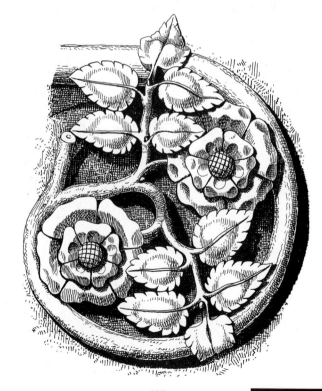

413

414

415

416

417

418

419

420

421

422

423

424

425

426

427

428

429

430

431

433

432

434

435

436

437

438

98

439

440

441

442

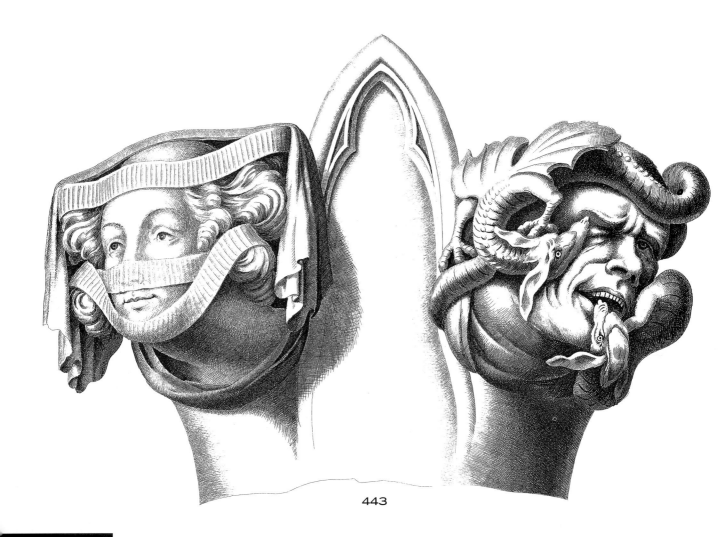

443

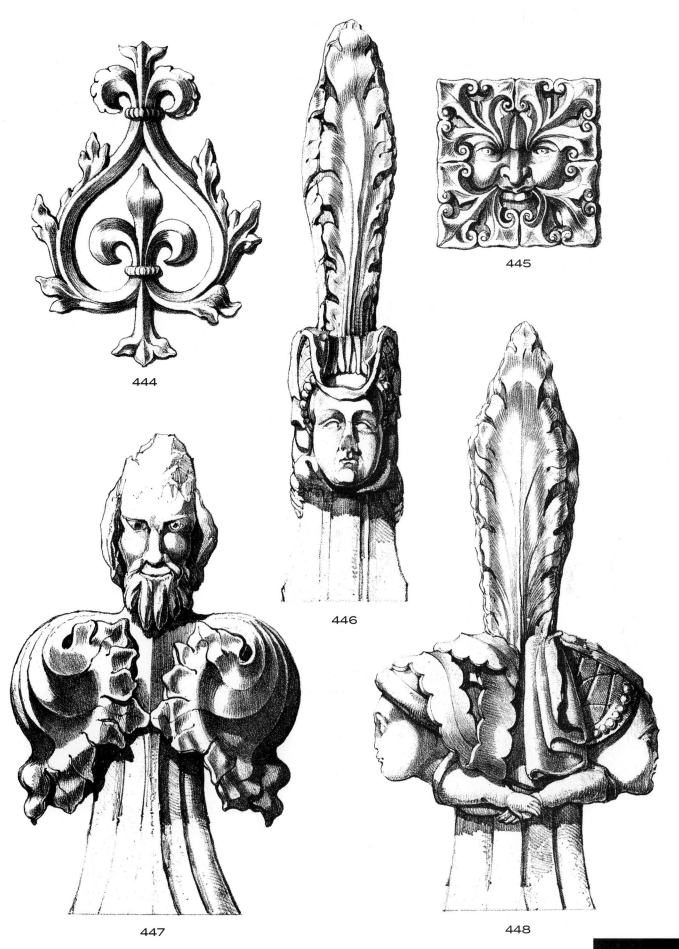

444

445

446

447

448

449

450

451

452

453

454

455

456

457

458

459

460

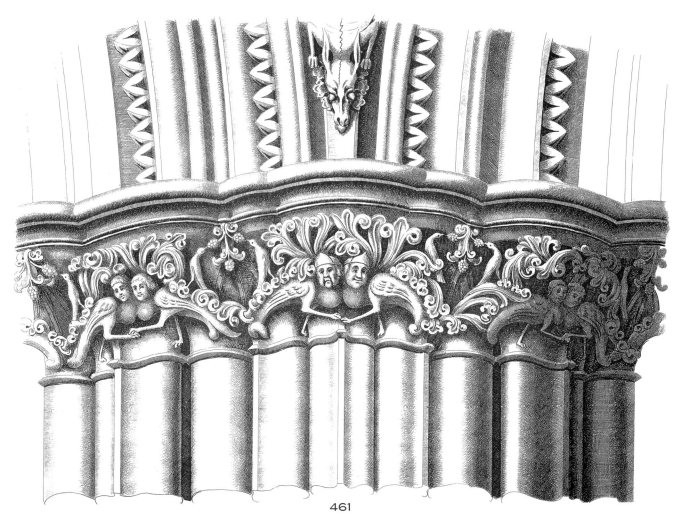

461

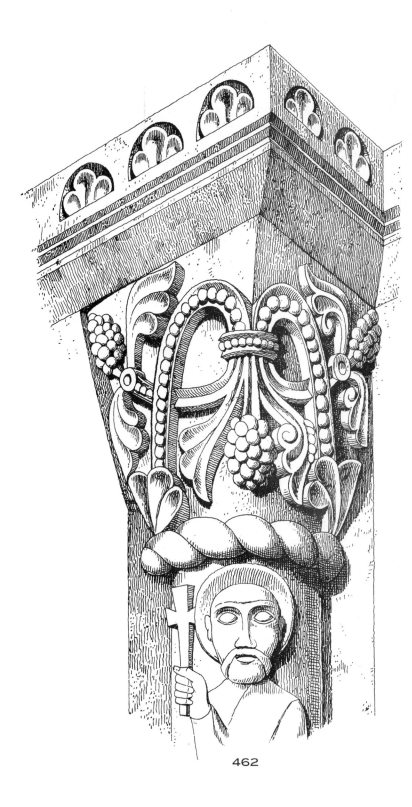

462

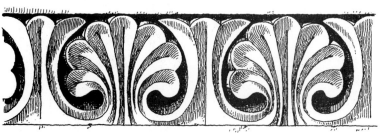

463

464

465

466

467

468

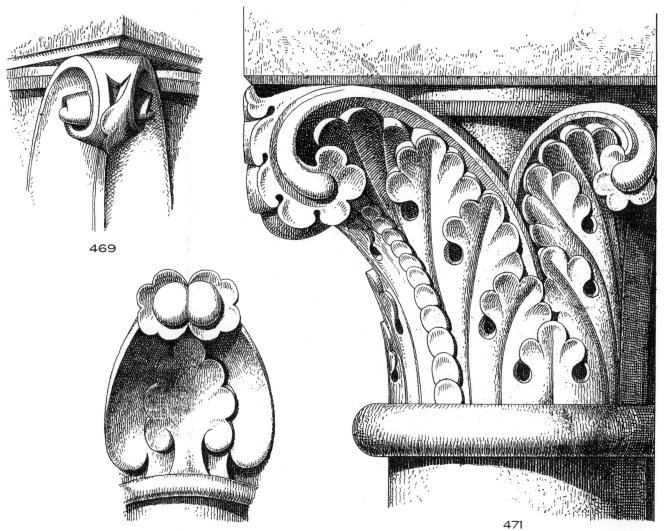

469

470

471

472

473

474

475

476

477

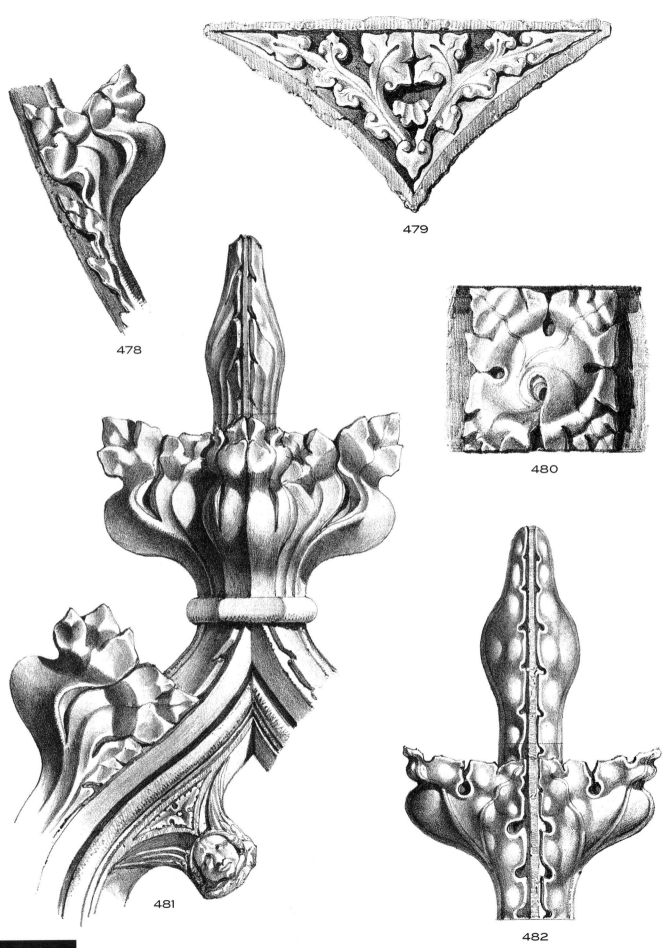

479

478

480

481

482

483

484   485

486

487

488

489

490

491

492

493

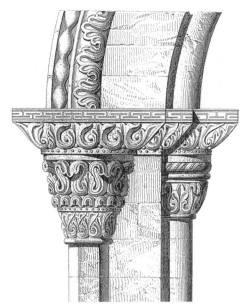

494

495

497

496

498

499

500

501

502

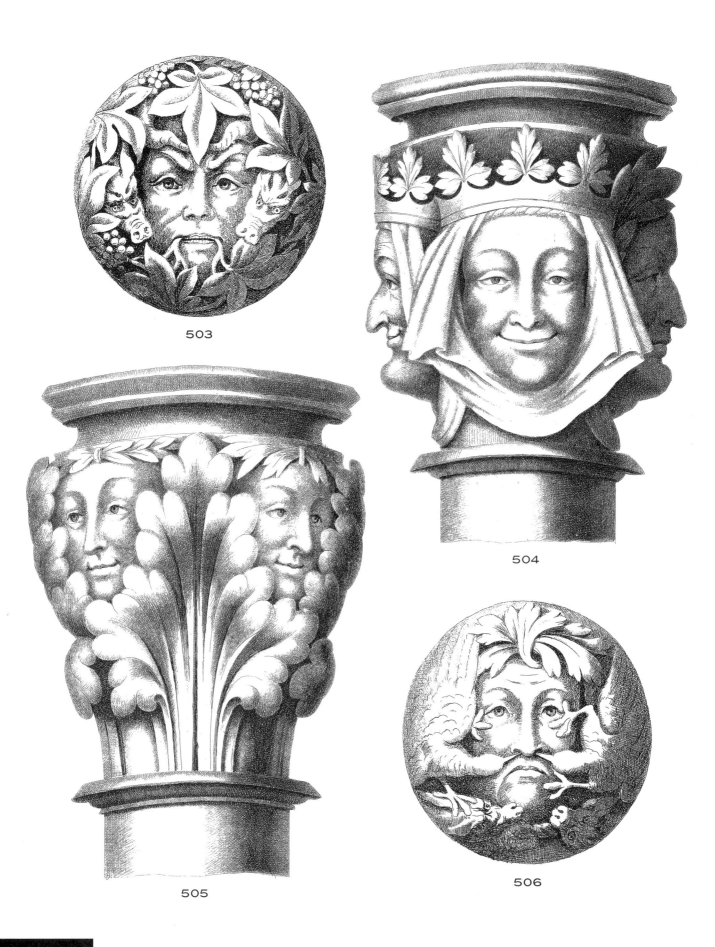

503

504

505

506

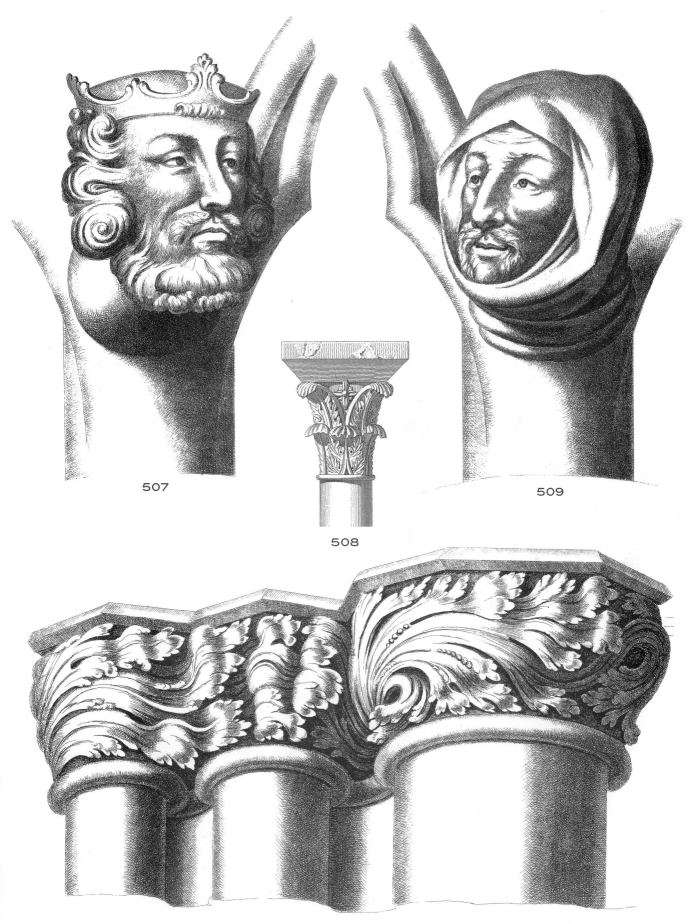

507

508

509

510

511

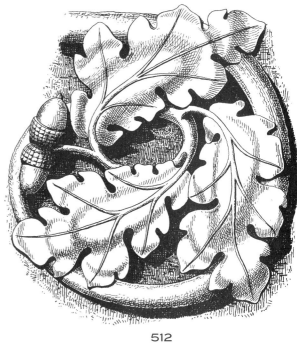

512

514

513

515

516

517

518

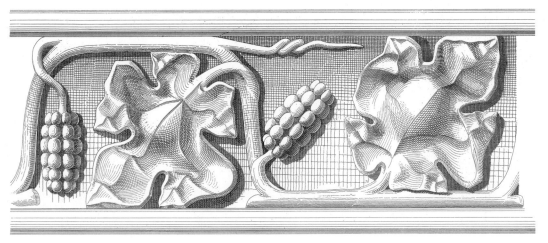

519

520

521

522

523

524

525

526

527

528

529

530

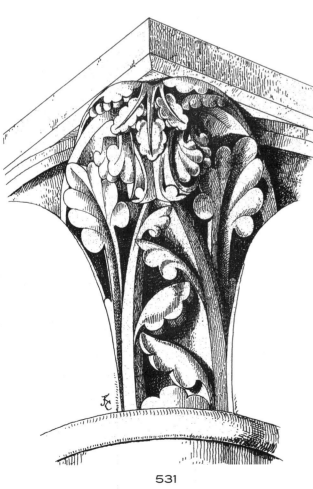

531

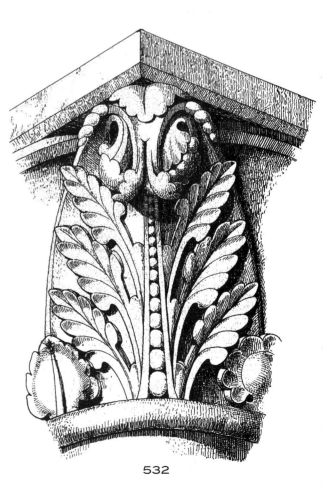

532

533

534

535

536

537